NIGHT VISION
The Poetry of Healing Military Sexual Trauma

NIGHT VISION
The Poetry of Healing Military Sexual Trauma

Amber Topp

DEDICATION

To those who tried to hold me down and those who came before me.

Library and Archives Canada Cataloguing in Publication
Topp, Amber author
Night Vision / Amber Topp

Issued in print and electronic formats.
ISBN: 978-1-990644-39-9 (soft cover)
ISBN: 978-1-990644-40-5 (e-book)

Editor: Phil Halton
Cover design: Pablo Javier Herrera
Interior Design: Winston A. Prescott

Double Dagger Books Ltd
Toronto, Ontario, Canada

www.doubledagger.ca

TABLE OF CONTENTS

FOREWORD

This book is made of the pieces of me I've left along the way, scattered in my often-chaotic wake. A feather here, a tattered piece of yarn there, fabric from the scarf you often used to wear. Like a mother bird made ready, I've gathered these pieces to nest for those to come.

Sometimes I pick up pieces from the dirt, a minuscule glimmer in the muck spotted from high above, I swoop low and dig, often uncovering a trove beneath, in places I never would have looked before. On other occasions a friend may offer me a piece from their borough, a coveted tuft of moss or blade of grass they had taken the time to bury for themselves, awaiting a season to share.

I take these pieces and mould them with clay, and branches, and blood from stones. I weave them, creating a tapestry, a soft blanket, a womb, a home.

I build my nest high, as a falcon would. Perched high above we better see our predators, and we protect each other, our treasures secure within our nest, our stories told.

I hope my pieces bring healing to your mind, voice to your truth, and fire to your soul. You can perch in my nest if you would like, or you may take a piece to build a nest of your own – before taking flight.

i

1

CRISP NOTES IN A DARK SKY

The Weight of the Clouds

That one kiss in the parking lot
An empty space
Snow falling in my hair
Frost forming on our lashes
An infinity
Forever ingrained
In the weight of the clouds
And the lines upon your face

Sandbox Games

Did we let this love destroy us
Playing silly games
I was on a seesaw
You were playing tag
Run away to your sandbox
Worry about your name
You put your gun before me
And watched me walk away

Icing

The icing dripped from my fingers
Sticky and sweet
Melting in the heat of the day

Relentless in the dark
It turned bitter
And regret couldn't wash it away

The Wave

The significance of the wave is as eternal as the rest of it all
The wave is my very soul, it is me, my very core
And you know me, this I can be sure
The wave speaks to that
The waves are my joy, my rejuvenation, my zen
The sound, how they crash, they are beautiful, they are
    constant
The wave is a paradigm of life

I saw the swell of it, it was more than my being knew
Jumping into it was powerful, an awakening to myself
Soaring to heights unknown, the saltwater taste in my mouth
Bittersweet, pungent, yet energizing and fresh
Refreshing, healing, awakening
This is me, I had forgotten

My heart had lay dormant, my being buried
The wave lifted me out, pulled me up from the depths
It raised me up, soaring in its crest
The wave healed me
With its salt, its flow, its depth

Yet the wave crashed down, as a wave should do
It smashed me in its power, it flowed over me
Then embraced me in its cool salty wake
It flowed back to the sea, as you said it would
And it left me broke, yet left me free, and kept me true
The wave left me scarred, yet worthy of the sea

Blood Spatter

I painted your name on the walls
Then I watched your blood spill out
Through the tears in the fabric of your being
Who knows the truth of what we are
Only you, and your mind is fleeting

Matchstick Girl

I refuse to apologize for my fire and ice heart
For the ice is my safe house
And my trauma operandi
If you want access to the fire, start warming up your
hands

Ode to My Baroness Heart

I hide within a mask of clay
A blanket to hide my carnivorous ways
I say to you, there's no love here at all
Only us
We've built mountains to keep it this way
In all our waking thoughts
We hide our thoughts away
I don't owe you anything
Yet you continue to say
My cold baroness heart
Cleaves pieces of you away

Wounded Tree

She left her blackened heart buried at wounded tree
For the roots to cradle and time to hold
For the cells to remember her truth

Ivy League

Even the ivy
Breathes your name
As it curls away from the sun
And every horizon wastes away
Corrupted by your touch

The Haunting

Who knows what is real
What was there may never be
What was true could be relieved
What was lies could be believed
Was it us in time of need
Did I need you to feel me
Did we cross a galaxy
Would our light shatter the sea
Could it keep
Should it be free
Was it real, was it me
Did I feel you in a breeze
Could I hear you in my sleep
Will I keep you in my dreams
Is a flame eternal need
I know I haunt you endlessly

Bound

He tells her that she's beautiful
With his hands over her face
He binds her wrists to his name
And burns the shame into her skin
A branding

She fathoms the thought of running
Breaking free of control and betrayal
But she confuses the empty pain of it
And the dissolution of what is real
A denial

That Which We Call Rose

Their name is Lieutenant
Their name is Corporal
Their name is private
Their name is forgotten

Their name is Sergeant
Their name is Warrant
Their name is Major
Their name is upheld

Their name is Morgan
Their name is Kendall
Their name is Avery
Their name is sustained

Their name is Alex
Their name is Jody
Their name is Rian
Their name is Overruled

Pale Horse

You ride around on your pale horse
With crisp shirts and guns blazing
All charisma and valour
Blinded by your own smile

I hope you see yourself
In all our words trailing
As they try to sweep
All your shit from the streets

And you come to terms
With the weight of your Denial

Shook

I'll tie you to the bed, he said
I'll scar your pretty face
I'll keep you in a heart-shaped box
And tarnish your good name

And when you tear the veil off
And dare to call my name
I'll flee the scene, hide from myself
To bathe my grief and shame

Crystal Ball

They tell us we are everything
Yet we are nothing
A crystal ball to be admired
Yet held up by a taunt string of power
I am strong and my glass can handle the pressure
If I wasn't a pillar of strength, I wouldn't be a soldier

This is how things are around here
Are you woman enough to play the game
Don't be weak
Don't be one of those girls

Nobody gets me like you do
My princess, my angel, my joy
I need you in my corner
My secret, my plaything, my toy

Soldiers don't tell
Soldiers don't speak
For we are, but of course
Not the weak

We carry on in a cage
Wrapped with ribbons and medals and bows
Still held tight by the string
For we all know
If the string breaks
It is us who shatter
Nothing more

Trigger Moon

It haunts me still
Washing over me like the tides
Ever pulled by the state of the moon

DNA

You've been here for years now
Imprinted in my DNA
The grains in the salt of the waves
Sometimes I wonder if you'll be here forever
And I know it will be that way
Like embers in the depths of a cage

Salt

Please don't speak to me of light
If you've never held the comfort of darkness
Wrapped in your cloak at night

Mourning Dove

I dive into the icy moors
Bathing in the grief of nevers
Washing away what was
Disoriented, my heart falters
And I wonder where I've been
Like Alice, I'll awaken from a dream
With the weight of realization
And the heights of madness
I'll never be what was
I'll never see the thaw of spring
Take me to the graveside of yesterday
To the wake of a bright future
To the films that portray love, and duty, and honour
Lay flowers at my feet, for I died here
In my sleep

The Little Things

Life is the little things
The writing on the walls
The dust along the floorboards
The spider in the hall

Love is the little things
The whisper in the wind
The tug of a heartstring
The melody within

Death is a little thing
The silence in the snow
The echo of a bang
The depths of the unknown

One of those Tracks

A note in this song is missing
The leaves continue to fall
And still, I wonder

My mind obsessed
Like a sieve sorting through memories
I pan for gold in the thrall

And the record skips a beat

The how, the why
The translucence of the sky
The ins, the outs
How this came about

Why didn't I stop it
Why wasn't it fixed
How do you weigh actions
Placing pieces where they fit

Maybe I deserved it
I villainize myself
Maybe this was my fault
I demonize myself

And the record skips a beat
And skips a beat
And skips a beat
And skips a beat...

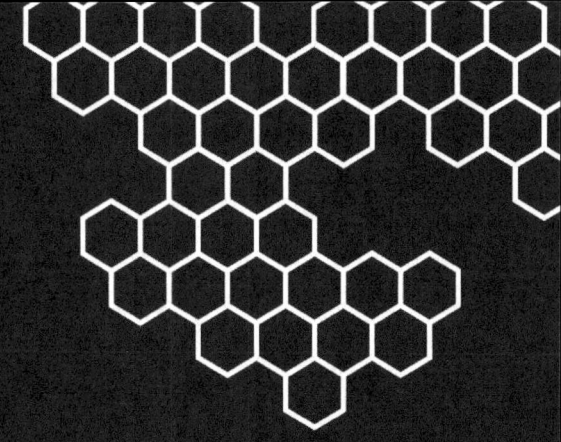

2

THE FORMATION OF CRYSTALS

Bowls

Sometimes you must accept that your bowl is already full
And put a cover on
To protect what is inside

Boundaries

I set my boundaries by the light of the moon
For now, I value myself

My peace, a gift given to me
Through the blood of my ancestors
A quiet strength, standing at the edge of an ocean
Absorbing the light all around

I am still, feeling the connections
I will never go back to less now

Sky Water

I am the rain
And when I'm thirsty, I realize myself
The sound of a distant drum
Culls me in
Deeper into the chasms of time
Sometimes in the sunrise I can see myself
Remembering the white doe's eyes
And sometimes when I'm alone I remember myself

Passion

Passion is the light of destiny
The fire in the well
That you feel after the dark
An accelerant ignited
By a calibrated spark

Empowered

In the night we are empowered
Our will united, we march
Our gaze straight, our heads held high
The glistening of our crowns never ceases

In the light we are empowered
Our hands clasped, we dance
Our feet raw, our eyes to the sky
The story of our song never ceasing

Morrighan

In her eyes they could feel her passion
The fire of Morrighan ignited in her veins
The voice of a thousand sisters dancing in her spark
And they all supported her heart on that mighty stage
As she spoke without fear of her dark

Night Witches

Here's your crown, witch of old, daughter of the night
Now blitz the earth beneath you
And watch your power ignite

Storytellers

We are the storytellers
Channeling words from the moon
Dancing with laughter
Etching history's tune

Red

No one knew how tenacious you were
Until you put on that dress, and commanded the room

A Valkyrie of wisdom and truth
Cast aside by those meant to be true

Carnelian Will

My will defeats your power
My song, your hollowed being
Your blackened steel won't bend me
I flow between your seams
I rise above this battleground
I'm heavy in the mist
I break apart, as thunder cracks
And crush you with my fist

Sacred Feminine

This is the sacred feminine
It is mine to wield as I please
Its power you will never control
Your words lay deaf at my feet
She will devour you into her chambers
Lose you in the depths of her heart
Eat your soul from the inside out
Birth you alone in the dark

Burn

But you are fickle in your soul
You brush the light off your shoulders
Like the dirt on your boots
Your flame is weak
You cannot control your shadows
Open the box, stop kicking, and eating all the fire
Just let it fucking burn you

Tigress

And she laughed in the face of her oppressors
For a tiger never loses her stripes
She simply lay in wait for them
All the while, within plain sight

Evergreen

I am evergreen
And I will stand towering over you
Long after you're forgotten
Taking in the divine light of the sun
My roots buried deep
In the sentiment of mother earth

Like the tendrils of a hawk gripping its prey
Embodying us all
Though you've torn at my bark
and stripped my branches bare in your darkness
I am light
My green never fades, through snow and sleet
I am mother, and small creatures seek my shelter

I am the voice in the wind
My core is strength
And your axe breaks within me, as I devour you whole
Never yielding
My voice is eternal
Echoing over future generations, like a mission bell

A red dress hanging from my boughs
A brass medal buried underneath

A wrinkle in time
A sailboat
A wisp
A candle
A heartbeat

Noose

She ate the sword for breakfast
As he held the noose in his hand

Limitless

We are limitless in our ability to heal
In our ability to see, to grow, to change
We are limitless in our love and compassion for one
    another
Our beauty bound together in the seasons
Our scars mending into one
Yes, we are limitless together
Limitless in peace, limitless in joy, limitless in courage
Yes, as one, we are limitless

Star Crossed

The light reflected off the water
And cut through the darkness
With the warmth of a blade
Through star-crossed ice

The Symphony

She stepped into the flow
And the universe surrounded her
In a kaleidoscope of life
As she raised her baton
To the symphony

The Glass Ceiling

As the glass shattered
I understood
That it had been beneath us all along

It was never above us
But always below

We just hadn't cleared the space to see it

Box of gold

She went into herself to find the wild
The root of peace within her soul
Maybe she was just too deep to hold
So vast, she appeared cold
Touch her for a moment to unfold
Always returning to herself
Safe in her box of gold

Flourish

She got up and walked away
From that closet
From that room
From that building
From that city
From that town

She emptied her pockets
And she walked away

From the judgment
From the expectations
From the control
From the shell

She walked away
And oh, my love, how she flourished

Leadership

After the length of the darkest night
My fight dwindling
I lay in the cold and fathomed
What it meant to be alone

My thoughts creeping
I swallowed my pride, deep in my gut
I ate my sorrow's longevity
For I knew in this moment, I must rise

He heard my story with a wounded face
My pain invoking a curse of his own
My final plea called out through the waves
My hope for rescue known

A strength dredged me up toward the light
Colours shimmering through the breaks
For I was heard, and for a moment, protected
I was cauterized

And I knew, that maybe,
Piece by piece
I could see myself realized

Spitfire

Whispers of change
Shift through the night

A melody of growth
A bedlam of rights

Through every anchor
And bright arc of light

We are people of fire
And we're still in the fight

Change

Delicate blossoms of change
Emerge from a cold dark heart
I wash the blood from my face
And prepare for a brand-new start

3

FOR THE SUN FEEDS US ALL

Intimately Grounded

The aroma of wild azaleas
Coffee freshly brewed
The earth solid beneath my seat
The heat of a star upon my face

A whimsical breeze within the air
The sand between my toes
The lap of rhythmic crystal waves
The cull of a meandering gull

Every beautiful essence before me
Reminding me I am here
Every sense of my chaotic soul
Reminding me I am intimately grounded

White Rabbit

She gazed through the pane
And beheld the white rabbit
His pelt glistening in the snow

And as she watched the winter
Thaw around him
She knew that she wasn't alone

Sunshine Cloud

Turn it around sunshine cloud
Command the winds and the haze
Own your heart in all its depths
Dive into the mists of your caves

The Light Within

And the light is within us all
In the layers underneath
Where the sun meets the sea
And the seconds in between

Hourglass

The hourglass of time knows us all
In the end, we are as one as the sand
Separate, yet apart

Connected in our collective weight
We are comforted by our essence
Every shade of being intertwined

Breaking through the glass
We are separated and consumed
For we are also the glass enclosing ourselves

Reflecting each other's light
We are conscious and true
Tiny grains of dirt exploding into sight

Dance of the Wandering Soul

Love, and angel dust, and chariots of fire
Eclipsed only by the desires our souls have transpired
Whims of heavenly thoughts and lucid dreams
Tripping through galaxies, never meant to be
Flowing through seasons of time
Then we rewind, and pass over the day
Where love was present, yet far away
Steeped in the sanctity of eternal thought
Darkness abandoned
Shadows only to remain for presenting the light
In the heights of withering refrains

Transcendence

This is transcendence
The light above the dark
Its weight simply rises
Only buoyed by the heart

Dark Horse

In the Windermere willows I watched the dark horse
    play
She jumped and leaped along the pines
Frolicking in the contrast between light and dark
A heavy heart pounding in her airy chest

She was searching for herself amongst the herd
In the contrast she was fleeting
But there were always glimpses floating around
In the wings of a dove or the smell of the dew

The dark horse heard her own voice break through
And she galloped into the space of light
Where she realized she was not a horse at all
Though she frolicked and played the same

She saw herself in the pale horse and the unicorn alike
And she remembered she was also the Pegasus
She felt herself shine through the power of the moon
And she rose to the call of the light

Wonders that Mark

Every dream,
Gentle whisper
Is a light within our arcs

The stillness of the soul
The nature of the heart
A moment in time

A breath
A beat
A spark

All the wonders that mark
The stars within the dark

The Stairs

One day I stood upon the stairs, and looked down
And I knew that I was found
Far from the earth
The molten stars surround me, owning the night sky
A lark sang in the open air
I washed it all away, with the well of my hand
I glimmered as if to show all who gleamed that I was
  there
Every galaxy was awake
I lay down in the celestial plain
And here we rest, for time has no place in the ancient of
  days

The Force

Can you feel the force
Ever flowing through our veins
Ever growing in the waves
Ever blowing through the trees
Can you feel the force

Can you feel the force
Ever beating like a drum
Ever rolling like a train
Ever eating through the sky
Can you feel the force

Fantastic Beings

But who are we
If not fantastic beings
Dancing on a molecular level
Like snowflakes floating through the sky
So do we all, through this magnificent life

Emberglow

I sat in the warmth of my cave
And I watched the flames dance
Until I found myself there
For many years I had huddled alone
Enclosed by my trauma and pain
The fire consumed me, before I arose
My heart song known, healed and whole
I held out my intricate hands
Awash in my own blood and decay
And I reignited the flames
With the light within my soul
The fire of my own heart

That was many moons ago
But in the embrace of the cave
The heat remains
And you can always find me there
An eternal emberglow

Magic

Touch your magic
And feel its heat embrace you
It's fire consume you
It's womb rebirth you

Unearth your power
And feel its strength redeem you
It's arms subdue you
It's gaze reclaim you

Replenished

Let's go on a journey
Where every drop of water
Is embellished like silk
Where we glitter like the diamonds we are

Let us lay in the grass
And wash our faces in the rain
Watch the flowers grow around us
Surrender ourselves to the day

4

DAHLIAS AT DAYBREAK

Siren

In the afterglow she basks
Like a mermaid on a rock
Or a siren on a boat
Maybe both

Beauty Smooth

Inject my face with youth
For true beauty lies within
But I want it to be smooth

Ice

The ice on the mountaintop shifted
And slid down
All the way down to the depths
And melted away
Into water
And nourished the roots of the well

Home

Dirt under my feet
The smell of wood and dew
Mist rising from an endless lake
A fire crackles
Its ashes rising in the air
The memories of carnal times

Your warmth surrounds me
Like a quilt of old
And I know that I am home

Thunder

I felt the thunder crack you open like a crypt
As your touch crumbled my walls

Etched

The heart equates love to a rip through time
Never knowing its true existence
Something so existential to the mind
Can only be felt in the realm of light
A twilight revolution in her face
She feels the power intertwine
Her heart beats forever in it's place
In the realm of forgotten signs

In Bloom

You placed your hands upon me, and I was in bloom
Your waters filling me up
Your sun igniting my sky
My soul rising up to meet you
My petals opening, wanting more
Starving for your enduring warmth

Lavish

He wrapped her in the warmth of his heart
And his love was lavish

Secure in the weight of his arms
His love was lavish

Connected by the light in their darks
Their love was lavish

Rock Steady

You are my beacon
To which I'll always come home
My ship in the raging sea
My warmth in the arctic snow

And for you, I'll be your North Star
Your compass to guide you
Your anchor wherever you roam

Daisy Fire

She cradled him through the dark
Her essence of daisies, and milk, and fire
Holding the demons at bay

They float together on an island
Fighting through each frothy wave

A stronghold built for each other
Of love, and peace, and strength

Mosaic Castle

They dug the earth together
Mixed the mortar, planed the land
They took all their damaged pieces
And mended them by hand

All the splintered cracks and damage
Carefully filled with curated sand
Each piece lovingly fit together
Built for any peril to withstand

A castle in the altitude
A fortress in the heights
A sanctuary of peace and heart
A lighthouse in the night

Manifest Flight

Everything I've ever wanted
Has come to me like flame
A warmth radiated by thought
A wealth manifested by light
A heat orbiting chaotic plains

Artists in the Coliseum

We are the artists
Writing the words between the lines
Painting the air behind the scenes
Playing the keys beneath the time

We live our lives
Bodies entrenched in the earth
Souls touching the sky
Suspended there we perch
Forever waiting for the divine

Acknowledgments

I would like to thank my husband, Patrick, without whose unwavering support and stalwart strength I would never have found the time, energy, or gumption to put this book together.

I would be remiss to not also thank the team at Double Dagger Books, for believing in a project that was vastly out of their comfort zone, but direly important to our culture. For believing in the importance of words and in bringing light to difficult subjects. Your support will forever change lives.

DOUBLE†DAGGER

— www.doubledagger.ca —

Double Dagger Books is Canada's only military-focused publisher. Conflict and warfare have shaped human history since before we began to record it. The earliest stories that we know of, passed on as oral tradition, speak of war, and more importantly, the essential elements of the human condition that are revealed under its pressure. We are dedicated to publishing material that, while rooted in conflict, transcends the idea of "war" as merely a genre. Fiction, non- fiction, and stuff that defies categorization, we want to read it all.

Because if you want peace, study war.

About the Author

Amber Topp is a currently serving member of the Canadian Armed Forces, as well as a military spouse of almost twenty years. She currently resides in Ontario with her husband and children. She is a graduate of the Loyalist College, Protection, Security, and Investigations program, in Belleville, ON, and studied at St Thomas University in Fredericton, NB. She has a long-standing history of working with women and children, has spent time volunteering at an orphanage in Guatemala, and has also led focus groups and workshops for girls, focusing on Intersecting sites of violence, self-esteem, and positive self-Image. Amber has a lifelong passion for writing and has been writing poetry for over twenty-five years.